The TRUTH About CATS

What Cats Do When You're Not Looking

MARY COLSON

Raintree is an imprint of Capstone Global Library Limited, a company incorporated in England and Wales having its registered office at 264 Banbury Road, Oxford, OX2 7DY – Registered company number: 6695582

www.raintree.co.uk
myorders@raintree.co.uk

Edited by Helen Cox Cannons
Designed by Philippa Jenkins
Picture research by Morgan Walters
Production by Laura Manthe
Originated by Capstone Global Library Limited
Printed and bound in India

ISBN 978 1 4747 3849 1 (hardback)
21 20 19 18 17
10 9 8 7 6 5 4 3 2 1

ISBN 978 1 4747 3853 8 (paperback)
22 21 20 19 18
10 9 8 7 6 5 4 3 2 1

British Library Cataloguing in Publication Data
A full catalogue record for this book is available from the British Library.

Acknowledgements
We would like to thank the following for permission to reproduce photographs: All photographs by Capstone Studio: Karon Duke; Shutterstock: (cat face) 19.

We would like to thank Ryan Neile from the Blue Cross animal charity for his invaluable help in the preparation of this book.

Disclaimer
All the internet addresses (URLs) given in this book were valid at the time of going to press. However, due to the dynamic nature of the internet, some addresses may have changed, or sites may have changed or ceased to exist since publication. While the author and publishers regret any inconvenience this may cause readers, no responsibility for any such changes can be accepted by either the author or the publishers.

In memory of Otis

Some words are shown in bold, **like this**. You can find out what they mean by looking in the glossary.

CONTENTS

Hello!

Meow! My name is Otis. It's simply splendid to meet you. I'm going to tell you all about myself and my many talents.

You will find I'm pretty incredible. I mean, look at me. Have you ever seen anything quite so purr-fect? I know I look silky smooth but I'm quite wild, really.

Breakfast time

I live with my owners, Anna and Ben, and their parents. As they get my breakfast, I rub against their legs. I put my **scent** on them to say that they are my friends. I have **scent glands** all over my body and lots in my chin and cheeks.

After everyone has left for school and work, I have a very busy day ahead of me.

Keeping clean

It takes a lot of cleaning to look this good! My tongue is rough, like sandpaper. I use it to clean off any dirt.

My own **scent** helps me to **communicate** with other cats. It tells them about who I am and where I've been.

Scratch attack!

That's better! I do love a good scratch. A sofa, a chair – anything will do!

I like to scratch against furniture to keep my claws short and sharp. I never know when I might need them! I even have my own **scratch post**.

Jumping high

Look at me jump! I am an amazing athlete. I can jump up to six times my own height in a single leap. Can you? Of course not! You're only a human.

We cats have super-strong **hind legs**. Our tails help us balance, too. I like to be high up to see what's going on.

Ready to attack

Behind all this fluff, I'm wild at heart. If I notice something such as a fly moving, I **stalk** it. Why do I do this? I'm hunting. I practise stalking all the time with my toys. I lie very still. I am very **patient**. I watch and wait until I am ready to attack.

Leaping into action

I have super-quick **reflexes** and very strong muscles. These help me to pounce on my **prey**. Got it!

My whiskers help me to hunt, too. They sense **vibrations** in the ground when prey is near. They also help me to judge space and distance. This is how I know whether I can squeeze through a gap.

Chasing away danger

Hiss! Hiss! Who's that outside the window? Get off my **patch**!

The fur on my back sticks up when I'm defending myself. My tail shows how I'm feeling, too. I swish my tail when I'm scared or angry. I'm a speedy runner if I'm chasing something.

Hiss! Go away!

What does my purr mean?

I purr when I'm being stroked by Anna or Ben. This means I'm happy. I also purr when I'm in pain or upset. If Anna or Ben stroke me when I'm sore, I scratch them. I don't mean to hurt them – it's a **reflex**.

Other kinds of cat such as lions and tigers can't purr. That's why pet cats like me are just purr-fect!

Time for a nap

We cats need our beauty sleep! Our busy lives are just *so* tiring. I can sleep anywhere. You might find me snoozing on your bed (or in other places I'm not supposed to be).

I sleep for at least 12 hours a day. I'm not always in a deep sleep, though. I'm always ready to leap up if danger is near!

Watching and waiting

Isn't it funny how I'm always at the door when you come home? I know you're coming, you see. My hearing is one of my superpowers! The shape of my ears means I can hear things long before humans can. I can also hear much higher noises than you can.

Hi, Anna and Ben! Meow!

When you go to sleep...

At night-time, I like to snoop around. I practise hunting at dawn and **dusk**. One of the many brilliant things about me is my eyes. My **pupils** are much bigger than yours. This means I can still see in places where there isn't much light.

In the morning, Anna and Ben find me snoozing in my bed. They don't know what I have been up to all night. A new day and a new adventure awaits!

How wild is *your* cat?

1. What does your cat do when it senses danger?

a) It licks its paws and starts cleaning itself.

b) It crouches down to hide away.

c) Its whiskers twitch and its fur stands up. It's ready to leap away!

2. What does your cat do when it sees another cat nearby?

a) It hides away in its basket.

b) It shows it isn't bothered and ignores it.

c) It watches and checks the new cat out. Sometimes it hisses.

3. How does your cat play with a toy mouse?

a) It pushes it under the sofa.

b) It sits and waits for it to do something.

c) It stalks it before pouncing on it and biting it.

4. What does your cat do to mark its patch?

a) It sleeps in as many places as possible.

b) It walks around a lot.

c) It rubs its cheeks and chin on you and the furniture. Now you all smell the same. You are in the gang!!

To find out how wild your cat is, check the results on page 32.

Glossary

communicate share information or feelings

dusk time of day after sunset when it is almost dark

hind legs back legs

patch territory; area where something lives or roams

patient able to stay calm and relaxed

prey animal hunted and eaten by another animal

pupils black spot in the middle of your eye

reflexes action that happens really fast without thinking about it

scent smell

scent glands special organs in the body that create smells

scratch post upright piece of wood covered with carpet for pets to scratch against

stalk sneak up on, with the aim of catching

vibrations tiny little movements like trembling

Find out more

Books

All About Cats and Kittens, Anita Ganeri (RSPCA, Scholastic, 2013)

Cats (Animal Family Albums), Charlotte Guillain (Raintree, 2014)

Cool Cat Projects (Pet Projects), Isabel Thomas (Raintree, 2015)

Kitty's Guide to Caring for Your Cat (Pets' Guides), Anita Ganeri (Raintree, 2013)

Websites

cats.org.uk
The Cats Protection League is the UK's leading cat charity. It helps around 200,000 cats and kittens every year. On its website you can find plenty of information about all cats, big and small.

www.rspca.org.uk
The Royal Society for the Prevention of Cruelty to Animals has lots of important information about pets and pet care.

Index

Quiz answers:

Mostly As: Are you sure that you have a cat and not a mouse? You've got the softest, tamest cat in the world!

Mostly Bs: Your cat is pretty wild. It likes to be active but isn't keen on facing up to danger.

Mostly Cs: Your cat is as wild as they come! It's ready to take on anything! In fact, it's just a whisker away from being a lion!